How to
Survive
Death

Niels Kjeldsen

How to Survive Death

Introduction

This is the story of my life, but, even more importantly, it may be the story of your life.

What I mean by the above statement will become clear as you read through these pages.

True, most chapters in this book are a description of my life. How interesting it will be is up to you to determine. Along with my life story, I should warn you that I dive into some pretty important wisdom in these pages, which I feel you will undoubtedly want to know at some point in life. I dare say the last chapter may contain some of the most important words you will ever read.

Answers to questions such as: "Does one continue to live after death?" and "What happens to people after they die?"

It is my reason for writing this book. I want to pass on to you the knowledge I have gathered from asking these big questions and supporting questions to help you in your life.

After death, whether the body is cremated or buried, we know that flesh perishes. But what about the spirit that animated the body, that gave it personality?

What happens to it after body death? Some call this entity that runs the body the *spirit* or *soul.*

Others use different names. How come there are so many different opinions about such an important subject? This is what I have covered in this book.

The awareness that one lives on after body death is nothing new. On the contrary, the further you go back in history, the more common knowledge it was that the soul survived death. Still today, millions of people in the world believe they have lived before this life and will continue to live. Studies show that more than 70% of the world's population know or believe in an afterlife. Ask "Doctor Google" if you do not believe me.

However, if you ask the people who believe in life after death what happens to them when they die, you will get vastly different opinions. Again, my reason for writing this book is to clarify where the soul goes after body death. Why does one want to know? Well, the way I look at it, when you reach a certain age or lose too many loved ones, death is sort of thrown in your face, like it or not. It makes it something worth knowing about, especially if death might not be as bad as you have been led to believe.

You might be thinking that you cannot possibly know what happens when you die; nobody knows, only God knows! Okay, but what *if* you could learn more? I mean, if there may be more to know, would you want to know?

You were not given an instruction book on how to live life when you were born, which means you were also not given instructions on how to handle the end of life properly.

Teaching does exist, however, and I will share the answers with you. In the last chapter, you will find body, mind, and spirit defined in detail with the appropriate references.

For the longest time, science has been unable to answer the spirit for the simple reason that the spirit is non-physical, and science primarily deals in the material universe. However, the technological age has finally advanced enough to prove that there is a spiritual aspect to life, and it can be measured.

For example, the idea of "out-of-body experience" is broadly accepted, but certainly not by everyone. Under the hands of psychiatrists, many people have been electroshocked in an attempt to "cure" those who claimed they had out-of-body experiences. It seems that parts of psychiatry are terrified of the idea that spiritual beings might exist who are not connected to a body. Fortunately, they are in the minority relative to the number of people on earth.

The last chapter of this book provides a precise explanation of what happens when your body dies and what you can and should do. I hope you will enjoy the journey with me as I describe the paths I have taken, the trouble I have gotten into, and the joy I have experienced in my life.

Growing up

We live, we survive, and we die. You can also say that a lifetime consists of a beginning, many changes, and an end. I started my journey in 1947, born Niels Kjeldsen. This body and name were both gifts from my parents, Ebba and Hans Kjeldsen. Like so many young people of that generation, my parents started messing around right after World War II. Nine months later, I arrived, a Baby Boomer. My parents also had another child, my sister Lis.

Growing up, my family and I lived in a suburb of Aarhus in Denmark. It was an idyllic peaceful place where everything was taken care of for little boys and girls, and everyone knew your name. My father was a bit of a craftsman who could do it all. He bought a house, dug out the basement, built a garage, and made rooms in the attic for little Niels and Lis.

Our grandma, Agnes, and grandpa, aka "The Boss," owned the inn shown in the photograph, Aarslev Inn. Agnes ran the kitchen that fed all the people who visited through the years. "The Boss" was a real gentleman. He seemed to create respect around him without even trying. It just came naturally. I guess that is why they called him "The Boss."

The Inn was situated near beautiful fields and a river that twisted and turned just below the road. Family get-togethers there was a blast for small irresponsible children, of which I was one.

Picture 1949. Aarslev Inn. Grandfather and grandmother.

My father, Hans, improved our house piece by piece; he and Ebba improved our lives little by little. As a driver for Esso, Hans drove gasoline to all the gas stations in Jutland. I was often included as an illegal passenger, an absolute joy for a 10-year-old. Oh, how tall and proud I would sit in that big tanker truck, looking down on other vehicles on the road as if they were toy cars.

Occasionally, the giant tanker un-loaded gasoline at private homes. We could call personal stops "perks," depending on your viewpoint. For me, it was all a great time, with no obligations and pure-play for many years. Mother Ebba worked part-time, so there was hot food every day.

The internal communication in the family, though, was nothing to write home about.

You can say we were an average fifties family. There was lots of food and good service, but little communication from my parents or relatives about what was important in life. Maybe that's because nothing was important to my parents; they just trudged on. I remember our first fridge. It seems like another lifetime. In Denmark in the early fifties, a refrigerator was something special, let me tell you. It even came with a key!

The neighbors next door to us picked up this other crazy invention, a black and white box that we would stare at all day. It was called a "television."

Mostly, for me, life as a child was a breeze. In the summer, I would spend my days playing soccer and baseball.

What joy. One winter, I got an electric toy car. It was a massive hit with all my friends.

But not everything was a breeze. Mr. Kjeldsen had the idea that children should work. Dad was old school; he firmly believed you had to produce something to receive something. Strange? I spent many an afternoon sweeping the street and mowing grass. Later I picked cucumbers for the gardener on the opposite side of the road from where we lived. It is how I made my very first 5 kroner (about 1 dollar), a large coin, which fit firmly in my hand, and my pocket. That was my pay for a week of hard work after school. I cherished that money.

My father won the lottery; it changed his and our lives. He decided to be a driving instructor and open Kjeldsen's Driving School. It became well known in Aarhus and the surrounding area and was his way of life up to retirement age.

All told, my childhood was pretty carefree. Although indeed, there were times when things got serious with my parents. My father could be rather stern; my mother did her share of worrying.

But the seriousness of life did not impinge on me until school started. Suddenly I had responsibilities, homework, deadlines, and I had to listen, listen, listen. Everyone agreed that it was all very important–too important, I felt at the time, and I still think this way today. Playing was not listed in the school curriculum.

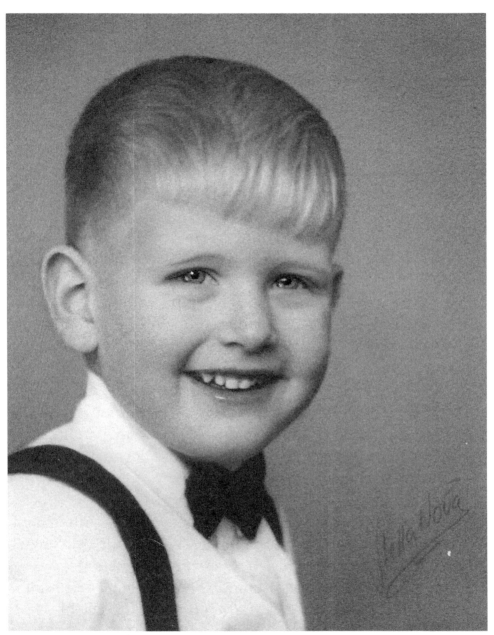

Niels Kjeldsen 1952.

Much later, as I grew up, I learned the art of taking it seriously without actually being serious. It is not a good state of mind to be too serious if you want to get things done. But that was not the mentality in and around the home in my youth.

Nevertheless, the school was a happy time up until the 5th grade. It was a downhill slide from there. I'll put it to you this way: there was little balance between the theory of what I learned in school and the practicality of how it was applied to life.

Everything was theory; very little practical application steps related to the real world. There were also many times I simply did not understand what was being taught. Later I learned that most of my confusion was merely not understanding some of the keywords that made up the subjects. Dictionaries are fabulous things, I have come to realize. Unfortunately, we never used them in the school I attended. I cannot remember ever looking up any words. I have no idea if there even was a dictionary in the classroom.

It is incredible to me that students graduated and went on to the university at all. We could all read and write, count a little bit, and that was about it. If you once raised your hand because you did not understand something, you would probably get made fun of; that would be the end of that. So instead of admitting you were ignorant by asking a dumb question, you would express your revenge on the teacher by making noise and causing trouble.

My school class. Aaby Skole, Denmark. I am in the second-to-last row, second from right.

The result for my friends and me was that we ended up causing trouble. And back then, you got beat up pretty good if you were a troublemaker.

At least three different teachers whacked me hard with a flat hand. Though, sometimes you had a choice between a slap to the face or being put in detention, staying in school an extra hour, doing nothing. I was the tough guy; I would choose a slap to the face.

One of the new teachers in school one year was a discus thrower, and when he put all his weight into a slap, it stung the rest of the day, and my ears would buzz. Even a tough guy like me could not pretend it did not hurt.

Another teacher jerked me across the gym by my hair. I am sure I did something wrong, but I cannot remember what.

Still, another punishment was to stand for an hour and stare at the corner of the room. Who thought that up? And finally, if you were terrible, you were sent to the School Principal to get multiple whacks on your rump with the cane.

Bad Boy Pranks and School Fatigue

The older we got, the more pranks and trouble we got in. The cane got bigger, and the penalties became more severe. It seems barbaric and old-fashioned to write about it in 2021, but in my neck of the woods in the fifties, whacking children was perfectly acceptable and legal. If fists started flying, teachers could lose their minds with anger and suffer no consequences from the school board or even parents.

When beaten by a teacher, you would never dream of complaining to your parents. You would only get told that "you earned it."

Once I made fun of a teacher. She went crazy and beat me with both hands until, in her hysteria, she could not hit anymore. Then she made me stare at the corner of the room for an hour. It did nothing but raise my status among classmates. Suddenly I became the guy who could take a beating without a reaction. That was quite a badge to wear.

Gert was one of my good friends. The son of a local junkyard scrapper, he was the top gun when it came to boy mischief at school. Somehow, he always had lots of money. At only 13, he would race to school on his tuned moped. Interesting, looking at it now, but it was fun to drive on tuned mopeds without a muffler. The louder, the better.

Like me, Gert found class boring. Together we suffered from school fatigue which manifested in plenty of troublemaking. Fortunately, there were no school psychologists at the time; otherwise, they would probably have stamped psych labels on us and plugged us full of drugs in a desperate attempt to settle us down.

Gert's mother had a grocery store. So, like the minor offenders we were, we stole beer she stored in the cellar. If she ever wondered where that beer went, we never heard. One time we hijacked his father's crane car and drove noisily across Aarhus up and down the main street to impress girls.

My confirmation. Father Hans and Mother Ebba.

We were only 16 at the time. You had to be 18 to get a driver's license. But we figured we drove better than most adults, so what the hell. After all, Gert had been driving his father's cars since he was 13, and driving instructor Hans Kjeldsen trained me.

My first encounter with a real weird personality was with Gert's big brother, Bruno. He was five years older and an actual criminal. He had no job and would continually squeeze money from his little brother and father.

For the record, Gert and I never stole to enrich ourselves; what we took here and there was illegal, yes, but only for fun. Bruno, on the other hand, was the real deal. Mostly he was a bully, a real jerk who liked to hang with Gert and me for some reason. Probably because we had fun, and he siphoned off our playful energy.

Anyway, everyone feared Bruno. He was bigger and stronger and meaner. Like all bullies, he was a master at intimidation. But one day, Bruno bullied the wrong guy.

He started knocking around his little brother Gert. I was older by then and had grown a few inches, and, well, let's just say it was payback time. I do not think Bruno ever bullied Gert again after I got through with him.

As time went on, I had hoped that Bruno had become a little more sensible. Wishful thinking. One day Bruno and I were standing in the junkyard workshop chatting. Bruno had a loaded air rifle. Yeah. He "accidentally" pushed the trigger, so it went off just over my foot. The pellet went through my rubber boots and into my big toe. I can still feel it today.

Bruno and even Gert's story is sad because the father, Soren, was as good as the day is long. He gave it all away to the sons without ever getting anything in return. It is interesting to look back at all this now; at the time, I did not know much about people like Bruno, but I have learned to spot his type of personality a mile away over the years.

I drove the family car every Sunday when we went traveling. Proud as a pope, I was, but not mother Ebba. She was mainly filled with anxiety with me behind the wheel. I also drove when the car needed to be cleaned on Saturday. My father was busy working hard at his job. He also worked at a local gas station for extra money.

My first real job was working at a car repair shop. A couple of drunken fun-loving mechanics taught me to drink beer and take apart a car, all at the same time. They would often send me across town on my bicycle to pick up car parts needed for a job.

Once, they sent me to get a car windshield. Imagine me carrying a windshield on my bike. I am lucky a strong gust of wind did not come along and drag me into the next town. There are laws against this sort of thing today, but hey, it was the early sixties then, and I was young and pretty naive.

Later I got a job with Mercedes in Aarhus, recommended by a family member in Copenhagen. I hated it. The mechanics were too serious, and the manager was a bizarre guy. Back then, we would say, "the vibes were bad." It was the only job I was ever fired from; I wasn't sorry about it one bit.

And then, there was my first sexual experience with the neighbor's daughter. Her name was Tove, and yes, she was the girl next door.

I would love to tell you how earth-shatteringly romantic it was, how it was a magical moment where my youthful innocence bloomed into full manhood in a breathtaking moment of eternal bliss. But you would know I was lying probably based on your own first experience. If I am, to be honest, it was a pretty sad affair—a somewhat awkward transition from self-satisfaction to real sex.

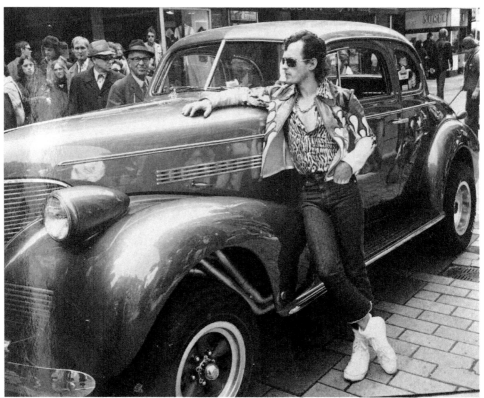

My friend AC in the sixties.

Sailor or Tourist

At sixteen years old, there was little planning in my life. To prove it, one day, my friend Leif suggested I take a trip with him on a large Norwegian tanker to see the world.

"Okay," I said. And just like that, I did it. The naivety of youth. The next thing I knew, we traveled to Liverpool, hopped on the boat, and were cruising the North Sea.

The ship personnel consisted of a diverse community of all different nationalities, an interesting lot. Dealing with the other languages and social habits on board was insane, especially during the hurricanes we would encounter. Keep reading. The captain and some of the crew were Norwegian, but most onboard were Chinese, South Americans, and Africans. Only some of them spoke English.

The journey was an adventure, for sure. It was also dangerous in many ways.

We sailed back and forth along the English coast several times and experienced a whole new culture starting at Liverpool. There were girls at every port ready to give one what one wanted.

Liverpool, UK.

You would think stopping in the English ports would be exciting. But not so much. Most of the ship people stopped at the first tavern they found on the dock and returned to the ship drunk shortly after that.

The officers on board were a little wiser. They went on excursions and experienced the different cultures available to them.

After a few months on the English west coast, we sailed across the Atlantic. First to the United States and then to southern Canada, where the 20,000-ton tanker cruised far inland on a giant deep river where there was no space for two ships at once. The crew fished for sharks while sailing there.

That was pretty exciting. Next, we were off to Venezuela, the Gulf of Maracaibo, where we spent time, and, without me knowing why, we sailed a lot around South America before heading back to Gibraltar. We ended up in Italy, where a large part of the crew was disembarked after fights with each other onboard, over what, I don't know to this day.

Sailing from Liverpool to the United States, we hit a hurricane in the Atlantic. The ship could not move forward for more than 24 hours. Everything was tied and lashed as we rode the storm. It was a hair-raising event. The boat tilted and rolled, and I was sick as a dog.

It was the worst trip I have ever experienced at sea. Ever. All I could think about was lying down and moaning, but there was no such thing while being a sailor. They forced me to run up and down, back and forth, to the engine room where I was doing the job of a machinist. But soon discovered I wasn't old enough to be a machinist. I was certainly big enough, and I had experience in mechanics, but they saw I was too young when they saw my papers. So, I ended up being an assistant in the machine room.

Believe it or not, I was given the assignment to paint in the engine room during the hurricane. There I stood, trying to keep my balance, paintbrush in hand, moaning and rocking and wishing I was elsewhere while the wind tossed the boat around.

You are probably thinking it made no sense to work doing something so insignificant under those circumstances, and you would be correct, but those were the rules. Sick or not, you had to work.

"Poor Niels," my mother would have said in sympathy if she had been there, but she was not. We made it through the hurricane.

I was young and cocky back then, and I did not back down from confrontations. I was also pretty good at boxing, which I was called to demonstrate one night in a camp.

Venezuela, where most of the sailors went when they had free time. The camp offered lots of easy-going girls who received money for well-done work. According to the rumors, they were examined by a doctor for possible illnesses, so everyone felt safe with them, kind of.

Our ship at anchor in Venezuela.

During the festivities on this particular night, an officer from our ship became physically abusive to one of the girls. I stepped in, and to his great surprise, as well as all the others who were present, that officer got "demoted" by me.

I saved the damsel in distress which won me a free trip to her private area for a treat. She put me in a room, locked the door, and left. Unfortunately, the time to return to the ship was fast approaching. Ships wait for no one, so I could not wait for her. Also, I could not get out of that blasted room. I panicked and started shouting for help from the other ship members who were out there.

The girl had planned to keep me for protection or whatever. I managed to get out and back to the ship in time. Thank God, or I still might be stuck in the camp in Venezuela.

In general, the atmosphere on board was not good. The deck crew drank everything from Aqua Velva (aftershave) to pure liquor to every other alcohol type they could find. It is amazing how creative a group of alcohol-thirsty sailors can get when they need a fix. Fighting would often break out just for the sake of action. I guess any game is better than no game.

For these primitive people, fighting and drinking were indeed games, but their subconscious minds mostly dictated them. In other words, there was nothing logical about their fighting and drinking. It was all out of control.

At one point, a small flock of men set out across the ship's bridge to kill the captain. I had not involved myself, thank you. Fortunately, they didn't accomplish their goal, and there was no mutiny or killings.

Leif, Niels, and Miguel on the ship.

Not long after that, many sailors were sent home. Leif and I decided it was time to go as well. We jumped off the ship and took the first train from Genoa in Italy back home to Aarhus.

In retrospect, my time on the ship was a great experience that I would never want to experience again. It was a mixture of good and bad, mostly bad, but it could have ended much worse.

Mid-ship on the tanker. The photo was taken with my Kodak click camera.

The positive takeaway was that we got to see Italy, Gibraltar, the USA, Canada, Venezuela, and several places in England. Not bad for two boys from Aarhus who had never been outside of Denmark.

We also took plenty of photos, whereas not one single person aboard did. Those photos are great to look at today.

Something about cars

I got an apprenticeship job as a car mechanic in the Auto Hall back in Aarhus. They were Renault dealers; the job was obtained through father Kjeldsen. I started in the gas station connected to the dealership, doing oil changes and taking care of the station in general.

Back then, we cleaned the car windshield of a customer who got a fill-up. Yep, there was more contact with people back in the sixties. I liked working there, except the man in charge often went off to drink beers with customers and mechanics. Like I said, more human contact.

My daily duty included fetching beers for the mechanics. Most of them liked to drink and were a lot of fun to be around. Oddly enough, the few who did not drink were very serious fellows and far less talkative.

I loved working with cars. Driving them in and out of the hall was a fun experience. I felt I was important with a boiler suit (coveralls) and a rag in my back pocket. A little later, I was transferred to the body shop department, some distance from the rest of the company. It was pretty much the same, lots of drinking during working hours and plenty of freedom to do what I wanted.

Cars. Shot by photographer and writer Thorsten Overgaard.

The leader of the body shop department was Kyfar, his nickname. He was good at straightening dents out, but he was a bit vicious when drinking, and he drank a lot. The assistant muttered to himself sometimes. During the breaks, the workers would play a game where we would hammer nails into a piece of wood. The first one to drive one nail all the way won. The poor guy who got his nail in last had to buy beer for everyone.

Occasionally, I would sneak out of my house at night and borrow one of the new cars. I would attach dealer plates and pick up my friends. They were impressed. That was a bad idea; it could have cost me my job, not to mention hefty fines. I was seventeen at the time and lived by the motto: "Who cares? If no one finds out, it is fine." My friends lived by the same slogan.

My "car borrowing" habit continued even outside my job. Father Kjeldsen had an extra car, which I went joyriding in when my parents were out. I continued to impress my friends. One night, Father Hans had the feeling that something was going on, so he had taken the license plates off the car. I wasn't going to let a little thing like that stop me. My friends and I raced around town without plates until an older gentleman in a Citroen followed us. Next thing you know, we were sliding sideways through the snow, trying to lose him. And we did lose him.

My father finally discovered what I was up to; he slapped me on the face hard, the only time dad ever laid hands on me. Taking his car put him in a pretty grumpy mood.

By that time, he was on the way out of the marriage with my mother and was unable to keep an eye on what was going on with any of us. Knowing he would not be with us much longer, I think he wanted to give me a message that I would not soon forget. My main protest was that he was leaving the family.

Did I mention that my borrowing car habit was terrible because I did not yet have my driver's license? In the EU, you have to be 18 to obtain a permit, even today.

Oh, the "funny ideas" I had that looked innocent at the time. The worst, or perhaps the funniest, was when I borrowed the number 10 bus depending on your point of view. The big bus ran from Aarhus city center to the terminus. The driver would often take a break at the bus station, get out of the bus, and leave it running.

I am sure neither he nor anyone else thought someone would be crazy enough to take it. But Niels was. One day, I had been at a party and had asked a few pretty girls if they wanted to be driven home on the bus. Talk about making an impression.

They said, "Yes!" I am sure they did not think I would do it. But I was well acquainted with vehicles from an early age so, when the driver got out of the bus, I perched myself in front of the steering wheel, practiced a little with the gear lever, and put the driver's seat in place. Then I said into the microphone, "Now we are running!"

Aboard were the pretty girls, six friends, and some regular passengers. Later, I discovered that the regular passengers had jumped out without my knowledge, even before releasing the clutch. I had forgotten to close the back door, and everyone used it as an escape route.

Bus # 10 in Aarhus, Denmark.

Off I went, driving the bus past three to four bus stops where people waited, wondering why the hell a kid was driving the bus wearing white girl shorts as a hat. (I was trying to look like an Arab.) I got no answers when I spoke into the microphone and asked which bar we should visit. I turned around and saw all 60 seats were empty. That is when the fun ended. I parked the bus and headed back to where I had started. Many of the people who had been on the bus were still there.

Some were pretty upset. Some had skin scrapes from when they jumped off the bus. Others thought it was pretty funny.

The pretty girls may have thought something was wrong with me. The next day, the police arrived at my workplace. The police officer said, "Do you know why we're here, son?" "No, sir," I replied. They explained that everyone in the area knew me. I confessed. I told them in detail how good I was at driving because my father was a driving instructor. I had been driving since I was a child.

On the way to the station, we stopped next to one of the big yellow buses at a stoplight. One of the police officers looked up at it and asked me from the front seat, "How did you dare take a bus?" I proudly explained to him how easy it was with power steering and how I quickly got used to the bus being much longer than a regular car, etc. One of the officers was a little impressed but tried not to show it.

It cost Mr. Kjeldsen a fat fine, and I was not allowed a driver's license the first year after I was eligible to drive.

From that day on, my nickname among my friends and the workplace was "Number 10." However, the bus incident finally ended the chapter of me borrowing cars.

Eventually, I quit my job at the auto shop to join my friends who were making good money welding garden furniture together. I liked that job. The company was called Homa, and it paid well. I worked hard for a few years and saved my money.

Soon, I got my first car, a 57 Chevrolet, a cool car.

Motorcycles and
Motorcycle Racing

My interest in motorcycles began earlier in my life by messing around with old bikes in the field behind the junkyard.

An older group of guys would also ride there. They had real motorcycles, and I would get trips on the back seat as a passenger. I clearly remember how wild and wonderful it felt when Big Joe turned the throttle. His Triumph stormed forward, my stomach lurched, and I loved it. The sensation was the force released while providing controlled speed.

1960-69 Triumph Bonneville.

Wow! One of the reasons for living is to experience these sensations from the body. It feels good.

And this is very much what I experienced on a motorcycle. You sit in the open and just enjoy nature, the road, the wind, and everything at once. There is a sense of freedom.

My first accident on a motorbike was as a passenger; it also became the worst ever, even after driving many professional motorcycle races for several years. I was fortunate to survive the accident.

Steve McQueen on his Triumph.

I had no helmet. Wearing one was considered wimpy. So, there we went racing through a famous turn on the road. The game was to see how fast you could get through that sharp turn. We were three machines and laying down completely, as a driver should when navigating such a quick turn. But the bike on which I was a passenger did not have much grip on his back tire.

We hit some gravel, and the bike dropped. The driver hung on, but I went flying off and slid forty feet on my ass and elbow. Then I hit a high curb with my shoulder and arm, flew up–and landed in some bushes. Ouch! I tried to stand up but fell back into the bushes.

I must have looked like someone was trying to exit the bush after somebody had tossed in grenade. There I lay with my ass hanging out through my pants and my leg showing through the torn-up pants. My whole body was hurting.

As I waited for the ambulance, one of the residents came and asked everyone standing around looking at me: "Is he not dead yet?" He was one of the many people who had seen the madmen bikers drive past with too much speed, and now he could finally get revenge with his sly remark. But it was understandable, from the point of view I have now.

After a couple of hours in the emergency room, I was sent home to moan. In retrospect, it could have gone much worse. But it was bad enough. Man, I was hurting for weeks. Road rash got a new meaning. It was a long time before I could walk normally and move my arm again.

The old saying: If you fall off your horse, just dust yourself off and climb back in the saddle. The same is true with motorcycles. My appetite for the two-wheelers was still there. The accident could not stop the enthusiasm. So, I got right back on as soon as I could walk. But the next time, I was the driver, not the passenger, spinning around on my new Triumph. Despite the accident, this period of my life was good. I had a new motorcycle and a nice car at the same time.

Life mainly consisted of motorcycles, girls, and parties. On weekends I took trips on my shiny machine with my buddies. Several Sundays in a row, we went to the speedway and dirt track races. Pure pleasure. Not much responsibility for anything but many treats.

Still living in Aarhus, we found a privately-owned racetrack in the next town over. A farmer who liked racing made a Speedway track on his land. Novices like me and professional racers could run on his track before the Sunday race.

We would ride homemade racers. They drove more advanced bikes on the speedway, specially tuned machines, 500cc and 750cc. They were running ordinary machines tuned to be racers. The frames were built to fit around the engines. It was a charming way to run because you had all the big brand bikes featured: BSA, Triumph, Norton, and later on, the Japanese machines. These races are similar to what we call Flat Track here in the USA.

In the beginning, I rode solo bikes only, but my interest eventually evolved to sidecars. Riding with two people was more accessible and more fun in many ways.

Remember Gert, the junkyard owner's son? It turned out his father, Soren, had been into motorsport in the past. He had won several races when he was younger. So, when Gert and I got interested, Soren backed us financially and otherwise. The two old street boys from grammar and middle school became the new constellation in the sidecar race.

28-29-6-69 Elling

Niels Kjeldsen and Gert Nielsen racing at Elling in Silkeborg, Denmark.

Frank Damgaard was a famous motorcycle racer. He won more races than anyone before or after him in the sidecar class. Gert and I bought his old sidecar machine.

These machines are tailor-made for those who drive them. The better they are made, the better utilization of horsepower. Frank helped get the machine adjusted to our size.

Frank was a complicated person, crazy in some areas, violent at times, but at the same time very humorous and always willing to help. He had the sense of what we called "gearhead." Similar slang that meant being a skilled technician and tuner. He raced many years before us and continued years after we stopped. His sidecar passenger, Henning, was quite pleasant; I believe that was Frank's only family.

Niels Kjeldsen and Gert Nielsen in the lead. Lovel, Denmark.

Gert and I ended up as both competitors and friends with Frank. He had a lot of respect for us for some reason. The first year Gert and I raced was in the junior division. There we won pretty much everything, well trained by Frank.

The following year we moved up to the senior class. These guys were fast. Gert and I were not leading the pack anymore. For the first few races, we were usually in the back of the field, eating dirt. When you have seven other sidecar teams ahead of you, all spraying dirt, it hits you with a splat!

Niels Kjeldsen (55) and Gert Nielsen passes Frank Damgaard and Henning (50) Copenhagen, Denmark.

But it did not take long before we were up in front. We won a total of 22 races over the six years. We won two Danish championships and took the bronze in another.

Gert and I became a famous team, very athletic and fast. In sidecar racing, you must be coordinated, and we were, even though we never talked about it.

We just naturally moved as one unit. "The wild men from Aarhus," a journalist once called us. The name stuck. We had blazingly long hair, which was not common for motorbike racers in 1969. It was an exciting time.

During the summer, we could practically live off our earnings. The atmosphere and excitement were quite a package. Racing is hard to replace with anything.

Most races held around 20,000 spectators. They took place on the well-known tracks Skive Travbane, Charlottenlund

Travbane, Lovelbanen, Korskrobanen, Ornedals track, the Fangel track, and Nisseringen. Most of these tracks still exist today, but the sidecar motor race is not seen much in Denmark these days, although they occur in other EU countries.

It is mainly the classic Speedway you see in Denmark now, which is incredibly exciting. I am still a big fan: beautiful, wild, and very entertaining stuff to this day.

This photo I took myself in Horsens, Denmark 2016.

In between

For six years, I lived for racing. But we only raced half of the year, so there was a lot of in-between time. In the winter, we jogged in the woods, and for a few years, I was doing boxing training in the winter. Gert and I participated in the tough physical workouts, insanely difficult. Once we were exhausted, the boxers started boxing. Fighters are in good physical condition; I can tell you that. Probably the most demanding sports training there is. We were in great shape.

In my first experience with the gloves on, I went with someone much younger than me but well-trained. After the kid had hit me ten times on the nose without me being able to return a single punch, I just wanted to kill him. But I soon learned that anger is not what classic boxing is about.

I made sure to make time for girl acquaintances in between. My first real girlfriend was Lotte. We had fun as long as it lasted, which wasn't long. Next was Lone. An adorable and lovely girl. Sorry to say, I wasn't very responsible at the time, so it also ended probably too quickly. Shortly after we split up, she told me she was pregnant, and so she was. I could not bring myself back into the relationship because of it, but I clearly should have taken more responsibility than I did. Nine months later, a beautiful baby was born. Lone took full responsibility, and I drifted off. I paid for childcare for the next 18 years. It was the least I could do.

Occasionally there were other exciting acquaintances. With my current attitude, I would categorize myself at that time as being promiscuous.

My casual attitude ended the moment I met Astrid. I first saw her at the disco Karavellen, smiling right there at the bar. A natural fusion. We were together for many years. Her intelligence and artistic attitude became a beautiful counterpart to the somewhat trivial mentality. She attended many of my races the last year I was active. Lovely girl who deserved it all, but I only delivered part of it.

I eventually got a job as a motorcycle mechanic. The opportunity came with Sejr Motorcycles. Owned by three brothers, one of whom is still running the business. One of the brothers, Erik, raced with me as a sidecar passenger those few times when Gert was not available. All three brothers were hardworking and fun to be around. Erik had a lovely family, and we had good times together. One of my first experiences with hashish was with Erik, his wife, and Astrid. It turned into an evening of reckless laughter—a liberating and relaxing experience.

There was never any smoking hashish before a race. The reaction time goes down sharply with the pot. It is not a handicap one wants in motorcycle racing. It is essential to be present, especially at the start, and all the way around. One tiny misstep and you get passed by; you have to be a little bit in the future to have a chance.

A girl and her motorbike.

We only had two severe crashes in the many races. Both could have been deadly, but luck was with the redhead, one of the many nicknames I had.

I spent lots of time with different tuners to get the most optimum performance from the engine. Experimenting with tires and small details here and there was part of it. Interesting to see how you can improve your reaction time. Being there in the present time and having no attention in the past is the way to go. Not allowing yourself to worry also helps a lot.

Motorcycle speedway was gaining popularity in Denmark. Of course, Ole Olsen was the World Champion, and the most famous racer on the track. We participated in many races where he was the star.

We commoners thought that Ole was a little arrogant. Maybe we were just envious. He did a lot for speedway racing and still does. But many people liked the sidecar class that we raced in. In some ways, it was more exciting than Speedway, always dramatic and close races.

I knew many of the speedway riders who were racing at the time. That resulted in trips to England early in the year to train and get in shape for the season.

It was a great experience to suddenly drive on the road's left side and speak broken English to the locals. But when we visited the pubs in the evening, the language was hardly a problem. The English taverns had their language that we all understood. Wonderful!

In between, I had a few experiences with Road Racing and Trial in the wintertime. Exciting experiences, but it was dirt-track, running sideways (drifting) that was the most fun.

Gert and I raced until he, as my sidecar man, could no longer be bothered. He had a wife and two young children, and they started taking all of his time.

We had been in "the ring" for 6 to 7 years. By this time, I was also ready for something different.

Speedway in the seventies.

Morocco

One year, Astrid and I decided to ride from Denmark to Morocco in Africa on holiday (2500 miles) with my friend Claes. He on his Honda, and me on my new Triumph 750 cc Bonneville.

Astrid and Claes in Morocco.

I had Astrid on the back seat, Claes' bike was packed with lots of gear. It was a very long two-wheel drive. Fun, but not so much when it rained.

The more stable Japanese brands were taking over from the English motorcycles at that time. But I was a big fan of the British models. Claes and I had made a bet on who could drive to South Morocco, well down in Africa, and back again without repairing the motorcycle in any way. Only oil change and chain adjustment, etc., were allowed.

As we rode the Autobahn in Germany, I lost the bet because my rear wheel bearing broke. When we got it replaced, it turned out, funny enough, that it was a Japanese bearing that sat in the back wheel of my English Triumph.

The rest of the ride went well until we hit the small roads in southern Spain. Suddenly, a pool of oil flowed all over the middle of a narrow bend that we could not see until we were on top of it. Shit! I always jokingly told Astrid that my first concern would be my bike if we got in trouble. It was not so when it happened.

We hit the oil patch, and the bike slid out from under us, and we hit the pavement. Even though I broke my collarbone, my first concern was Astrid. It turned out that she had only a few abrasions and scratches.

My next concern was Claes. He was a fair distance behind us, so I crawled out of the oil pool to warn him. I heard him heading into the swing.

I got his attention enough that he lowered his speed, but still, the bike skidded on the oil, and he had to lay the bike down. Fortunately, he was not hurt.

We got ourselves pulled together. By now, my collarbone was killing me. It was broken in such a way that two bone pieces sat on top of each other.

We expected the following motorist to come by, would stop and help us. Instead, they slowed down just enough to curse at us in Spanish and then drove on.

Three more cars also passed us by before an elderly gentleman arrived in his Fiat, spun around in the big oil pool, and stopped and asked if he could help.

He took us to the nearest small town where there was no hospital but a private doctor who spoke only a little English. He tried to push my collarbone back in place by putting a knee in my back and yank on my shoulders.

The pain was unbearable. After a while, he got tired of my wailing and Astrid's crying. He shouted something in Spanish, and the nurse came with a giant syringe of morphine. It did not take long for me not to feel any pain.

I felt like I had wings. The doctors pushing and pulling on my collarbone did not hurt anymore. He finally got it in place. It was a new experience for me.

Even though I had experimented with drugs, I had never tried or wanted hard drugs. It was amazing. You almost do not feel the body, but you are still there experiencing it all. I suddenly realized how people could escape from it all with that sort of drug.

Niels Kjeldsen in Morocco Mountains.

Next, we had to find a hotel and stay there for a few days. The doctor had ordered me to fly home and send the motorcycle home, but that would not be the case; we had just started the journey. I was already having the bike repaired; it took some work. The headlight was broken, and the front fender could not be fixed. Nevertheless, we got it up and running again.

It turned out to be a mistake not to stay longer and wait for the collarbone to heal. The side streets of the Morocco cities are not like other civilized places, and without lights at night, things go wrong. Niels Kjeldsen's impatience cost him dearly.

In Marrakesh, I drove into a hole in the street. My collarbone slid out of place again; the bones once more sat on top of each other. At present, the bones are still on top of each other.

The Market in Marrakesh.

It hurt for a few days, but then we continued on our trip and experienced this whole new place, which was very different from Denmark. We were not the ones to go to a tourist agency and get directions for the new environment. We had the attitude that we take it as it comes and could adjust as needed. And as you can see, many adjustments were required.

We ate what they sold in the open markets, which gave interesting sensations that you would prefer to be without. The places where we lived had "standing" toilets. Not much help when you had an upset stomach after a lousy meal, of which we had a few.

Morocco has a beautiful beach. We took the whole ride up the coast, first to Rabat and then Casablanca. Then we drove inland to visit the Ketama mountains, where they cultivated cannabis. We were curious to see how the plants looked and how they were grown.

It was interesting; there was no running water and no electricity. The people there invited us in for food. The proud and friendly way they served us made it almost impossible to say no.

We became friends with the farmers and were able to purchase cannabis. Down there, you can smoke whatever you like, much different than Demark, where it was strictly forbidden. It was not allowed in Spain either, one of the countries we went through.

When I had the rear wheel removed from my bike in Germany for maintenance, I noticed a cavity in the hub. Why not stash the cannabis there? I did, and there was no problem going through Spain or any other country.

We had traveled up the coast to Tangier, where a ferry took us over to Spain. It was the only place where you could cross the water in that part of Africa. The ride home went fine, even without light and no front fender. I ate a lot of dirt and rain from the road. But that was alright.

We finally arrived home happy and in one piece (well, almost in one piece.) It had been a long and fascinating trip.

Self-discovery in Spain

Back home, my life became very loose. I didn't have much work and pushed Astrid out of my life. I did regret it, but then it was too late. I did not think I could love somebody else again. The black demons closed in, and I lost confidence in myself. It seems like the way one drives oneself down is doing something that you know is wrong. I did not see it then, but I do now.

I had many friends and made even more when I attended training courses to drive bulldozers, tractors, backhoes, and the like. During my stay at that training facility, I got to know some academics who were without work.

They played music together, cultivated their vegetables, and were like weekend hippies. It gave me a new perspective. When I blended these academics with my old motorcycle friends, it created a fun atmosphere.

They most had in common that they all liked parties, pot, and beer. The learned young people thought it was fun to be with us "ordinary folks" who did not have their reserved and snotty speaking ways.

They were not used to people being so straight. They liked it.

Stinne and Christoffer in 1990.

It also became an experience to live in a collective environment. We rented a cozy place outside the town in the countryside. We had an entire house that was connected to a horseback riding school. Benny lived in the stables with the horses. He ran the place.

I had to try horseback riding. You are in pretty good shape when you have "ridden" motorcycles for 20 years; I figured managing an animal should not be a problem.

I bet you can guess where this is going. After receiving a whopping 5 minutes of instruction from Benny, I mounted the monster. We walked. We cantered. No problem. Then we hit the hills, and the four-legged beast took off, but where are the brakes! I think the animal was trying to tell me something - like who the boss is. Somehow, I managed to stay in the saddle. But not all the other riders did that day. A few fell off their steeds. Fortunately, no one was hurt badly, but for Kjeldsen, it was the first and last ride.

I stayed at the training center for a year. Collective living, I learned, was not the best for me, but it was a good experience, nonetheless.

The trip to Morocco had created ideas in my mind. Observing that people who smoked pot got calmer and more even-tempered, I became convinced (don't laugh) that it was suitable for people, especially compared to the pills and alcohol that so many indulged in.

So, when I arrived in southern Spain and lived there for a year, I lived a wild and relaxed lifestyle that included more indulgence in drugs than I would like to admit.

Spain, as many people know it.

The "mañana" (do it tomorrow) attitude fits the time and place very well. Many Danes and many other nationalities lived in the area, sharing experiences and cultures. I got pretty good at speaking English that year.

While in Spain, it was not difficult to get to Morocco when we needed supplies. We called it a mind-expanding substance. The "supplies" could raise your consciousness, so it did for me.

One day, after a couple of hash cakes and some other goods, I noticed someone sitting on a bench. There was something mysterious about this fellow. He looked a lot like me. It took some time before I figured out that it was ME.

I had seen myself from outside of my body. Even though drugs produced the experience, I saw the body quite clearly from outside of it.

In the Frostrup festival earlier, I had had the same out-of-body experience, but at that time, I did not know if it was a hallucination or if it had happened.

The Frostrup camp was a kind of youth rebellion place. Some would call it a hippie sanctuary. But there was brilliant music and lots of people. I was there only once, slept in a tent for a few days.

After a few out-of-body experiences, I became very interested in the spiritual side of life. I saw it as the way forward. Also, I noticed that hashish and other drugs were not the things to do. I had been experiencing a chemical release with those things, which is real, but at the same time, not the real thing.

I started reading a lot of books, searching and eager for knowledge.

At the same time, I had friends smoking pot, taking speed and cocaine, and other drugs to feel better. It was a way to forget your problems, basically the same reasons that make people drink.

But there were those of us who were interested in greater awareness and understanding of life. I and some of my friends read all kinds of philosophies and theories.

At one point in Spain, I heard rumors of something new in England. A couple of well-known music groups, including the Incredible String Band, talked about "the natural high." The group members had been taking drugs but found other methods to obtain even better states of mind.

Without taking any substances, I heard they could achieve higher awareness; I was looking for that exact thing. I did not think much about it at the time. Later, I found that the new movement they were talking about was Scientology®.

Christiania in Copenhagen, Denmark.

The town of Christiania in Denmark was blooming at that time. It was the ultimate hippie hangout. So, one of the first things I did after Spain was to visit the place. A free town in the middle of Copenhagen, interesting concept.

It got international recognition and is still famous. The atmosphere and music were super. Many well-known groups played there.

I think it started with a noble idea, to be free, but as soon as hard drugs and pushers got in there, the charm was quickly lost.

Most people saw Christiania as an experiment: Could a group of people live for free, not paying for anything, not part of the normal society? It seemed to work, to a degree, for a long time.

Scientology: Game Changer

The visit to Spain became the basis for later success and significant changes in my life. My friend Claes sent me books written by L. Ron Hubbard®, the founder of Scientology. I read them with great interest, in addition to the many other well-known philosophers.

Some months after returning home, Claes told me some friends had launched a small center in Aarhus. It was established by two sisters, whom I had met once before. The small group was located in Graven in Aarhus.

The two sisters had started the center from scratch. There was no money for large buildings like you see now. They rented a small place.

The sisters themselves had achieved significant changes in their lives with these techniques. They were interested in others getting similar gains; that was their simple motivation. In truth, they were brilliant examples of how it worked. Both had a natural radiance and were very easy to talk to; there was nothing wrong with their looks either.

Graven in Aarhus, Denmark.

It wasn't long before I took the formidable Communication Course®. I needed it, and it turned out to be great for me!

"Communication is life. One's ability to communicate can spell the difference between success or failure in all aspects of living. You will notice that those people you know who are successful in their endeavors generally have a high ability to communicate; those who are not, do not." L. Ron Hubbard. (1)

With gradual learning and application, you come up to a point where your outlook on life changes. You practice until there is no uncomfortableness at all. Wonderful!

With simple exercises, I was suddenly far more positive and interested in other people. A classic course in Scientology that has improved the lives of thousands of people. Millions if you look at it worldwide. It made so much sense to me.

Everything in my life changed. I went from chasing girls, drinking, smoking pot, motorcycles, and so on to become a productive person who did solid work, drank very little, and had a great interest in improving myself—no more pot ever again after that. You do not need it.

When you start to improve yourself, something else interesting happens too. You suddenly have an urge to help others. Something entirely new for me. Before, it was just what I could get out of things. Now, I was more interested in how I could assist others.

It was a new day for Niels Kjeldsen, who had lived in ignorance until then, to be honest. I had little interest in learning what I did not know for most of my life.
That practically changed overnight. Just learning a little of what they had to offer, I started to see the world differently.

From my perspective today, it seems to me that most people lie to themselves, pretending they are in control of their life when, to a large degree, they aren't. It takes insight and courage to acknowledge that you don't know things. That was how it was for me, so today, I easily understand other people when I talk to them about their lives and problems.

That out-of-body experience I had, set things in motion. How could I be entirely outside my body yet still control it? What is life really about? I had asked myself. Mr. Hubbard explains out-of-body experiences in simple terms that make complete sense.

The more I studied, the more I understood life. And it all started with the communication course. Those exercises did put things in perspective for me.

In his books, Hubbard explains what the mind is and how it relates to the body and spiritual side of life. Finally, there was someone who knew what he was talking about.

Niels Kjeldsen giving a speech in 1988.

At that time in my life, I had a deep appreciation for these books.

Previously, I had read tons of books from wise people like Dostoevsky, Herman Hesse, Carlos Castaneda, and many religious leaders who claimed to have answers. And yes, I also read parts of the Bible. So many men and women knew a lot, but it was all philosophical or theoretical.

Scientology was much more scientific and practical. It presented real "nuts and bolts" wisdom that got applied directly to my life. I could see, feel and experience the truth in what I learned immediately. Wow! In other words, it *worked*.

Again, I had delved into enough books previously to judge what had value and what did not make a real difference in my life. You could see if the data you learned was accurate or not.

Additionally, when I had studied the other Eastern philosophies, I ran across the Veda, ancient knowledge, and wisdom. Then I knew I was on to something big.

"SCIENTOLOGY is the science of knowing how to know answers. It is a wisdom in the tradition of ten thousand years of search in Asia and Western civilization. It is the Science of Human Affairs which treats the livingness and beingness of Man and demonstrates to him a pathway to greater freedom. Subjects which were consulted in the organization and development of Scientology include the *Veda*..." L. Ron Hubbard. (2)

What I am saying may be difficult to understand if you have not been acquainted with the subject. How can one change so much for the better in such a short time? Does it happen, or is it something the person imagines? I can only say that when something works for you, you know it altogether.

Today, many thousands of courses are routinely delivered in every corner of the globe. The workability of techniques is no longer a question. But back in the day, and as with embarking on anything new, it can seem a little daunting at first. That wasn't the case for me then or now. When you get down to it, it is simply about understanding life and applying knowledge to better one's life.

A mechanic that understands every part of an engine and each component's function can dismantle the entire machine, reassemble it, and, if he knows what he's doing, get it to run better.

He knows all the parts and what each piece is supposed to do and how it works. Similarly, if you understand the spirit and the mind, you can also do something with it.

For all the wisdom in the world, before Mr. Hubbard's research, there just had not been many others who had communicated the entire understanding of life and its parts.

If they knew, they would not electroshock people or give them pills for lack of confidence, depression, fear of the dark, fear of flying, and for hundreds of other bad experiences people encounter. They would just help people better handle their lives.

I am trying to tell you that it is not as complicated and challenging as you have been told. If you go to a dentist, he won't start experimenting with you; try this or that. Instead, he examines your mouth and fixes the problem.

In the same way with the mind and spirit, you can do something about it if you understand it.

As often happens when someone starts to better oneself, a few people around me would have preferred to keep the old ignorant and gloomy Niels, but it was too late. The train was leaving, and I was aboard. I could taste spiritual freedom. Order had come into my life. I applied common sense, and suddenly I had plans and goals for a new me.

Strandvejen in Aarhus, Denmark.

Looking back before, it was like I had been walking around in a maze, not knowing where to go, where I was, and how to get out. That was how it seemed to me in retrospect.

Suddenly, I was shown the route out of the maze. When one experiences daily restraint, lack of confidence, and dark thoughts and then suddenly, bang–almost just the opposite, well, one would have to be crazy not to continue on that path. So that's what I did. I was offered a way out, and I took it.

After reading and applying what I had learned in Scientology, I discovered I was no longer interested in getting stoned and doing other insane things. I was now positive and active, so it was expected that when one start to do well, some would make me wrong, and keep me down, or at least try. Respect came up quickly, however.

Niels Kjeldsen with his daughter and a friend.

It soon became apparent that I was doing very well. Even the most pessimistic could see I was more positive and more responsible in my actions. Suddenly I liked other people a lot, and I could enjoy life without a synthetic drug high.

All my closest friends and family joined me and did the Communication Course. They wanted to see what caused my zeal and change for the better.

Order became the keyword, order in life, order in communication. There was great joy in cleaning up all the old incomplete actions and helping others was suddenly something that made me extremely happy.

You have probably experienced people that influence you badly, others that don't make much difference in your life, then some that pull you up, and you feel better around them. I became one of the latter kinds of people.

We all feel better around people who are optimistic. Put another way: negative and hostile people are contagious, but so are those who are upbeat and friendly. In my new group, most people were cheerful and friendly.

They found solutions to problems rather than being the problem. It was fun to be with them. Many of the people in the groups I had hung with previously were sarcastic, derogatory, and quick to point out each other's weaknesses. Suddenly things were completely different. It was a great feeling!

In religious terms, one would call this a sort of revelation. But it was even better than that. In simple terms, I had found out that Scientology improves abilities, understanding, and knowledge. I was getting a solid idea of what it was all about. Pieces of the puzzle were falling into place.

Trine

I had met her before my trip to Spain. We were sitting in my yard. There were maybe four, five motorcycle enthusiasts, some drinking beer, others polishing their gear, and others showing off their latest new equipment. Everything was calm and cozy. And then a wonderful, bright, healthy-looking girl came driving in on her damn Vespa.

Scooters were vehicles we usually made fun of, but Trine was fresh and had personality. Something I was attracted to. She had another boyfriend at the time. I stayed clear because he was part of the gang.

After a few years passed, I was wildly impressed with Scientology's techniques, so I told everyone about it who would listen. I invited people to lectures, both friends with an academic background and those from the old motorcycle gang. And yes, even the family.

Most of them, it turned out, were not that interested. At the time, this was incomprehensible to me. With all the gains I had received in a short time, it seemed like a true enigma. Maybe it was because I led them toward the improvement rather than discovering it for themselves, I thought. I found out later that people have to have a particular awareness before they want to change.

Trine and Stinne at mid-summer celebration in Copenhagen.

Trine was the exception. She came into the center and was introduced to the Dianetics® book, which she read over the weekend. Afterward, she said of the book that she was interested if even half of it was true.

From my first perception of her years earlier in my yard, I thought Trine was a diamond in the rough. Funny how my perception turned out to be correct.

We hooked up, and I moved into her small apartment in downtown Aarhus. We got along excellent, but there were times that I spent more time doing life improvement courses than with her which she complained about a bit.

The technologies had changed my life so much, and it promised to change me for the better even more. I could not turn my back on it for anything. If I did, it would be like turning my back on myself. We had to adjust to life as a family and do ordinary things at the same time. We did this by using tools that you find in the basic books. Trine became even more dedicated than me.

After I went to a more advanced organization in Copenhagen and had some counseling, we moved there. The organization in Aarhus did not offer the more advanced courses that I wanted to take. So, we took our daughter Stinne and moved to Copenhagen.

In the beginning, Trine and I both worked as hourly employees, but it didn't take long before I got a job as a salesman and was able to make some real money.

Trine and Stinne outside the Blomster Café in Copenhagen.

Trine got the idea to start a florist shop in the center of Copenhagen, even though there were many other florists in the area. Virtually everyone thought it was a death sentence because she knew little about flowers, but she liked them and was a very creative person.

She started the Flower Café. I made deliveries for her in my spare time. It was before GPS and damn annoying, but the flowers reached their destination. Trine worked hard and eventually built up the business.

Trine and Niels in the Blomster Café, Copenhagen.

It became popular and ran successfully for a few years. Friends and customers had many pleasant moments in the Flower Cafe.

As Trine moved up the various stages of Scientology, she took on more and more responsibility. She decided to start a center in Copenhagen to inform people about it and deliver services. She sold the Flower Cafe and used the money to start the new project.

Copenhagen City Mission (CC Mission) it was called. It delivered courses on getting more control of one's life, improving relationships, improving one's learning skills, and the like. It was a huge success. I wasn't the only one who liked Trine–pretty much everyone did. She walked straight into people's hearts–you could say.

Her charm was natural and contagious. Her great interest in helping others made CC Mission one of the best functioning centers in Europe.

All our energy was spent on promoting and expanding the center. Many great new people came in. The team that worked there were able people who had made lots of gains from these principles. It was a good time for the Kjeldsen family, and Trine was the focal point. She was the founder of that group and kept it alive in her straightforward and direct manner. People came in from everywhere to get service there.

Trine and I eventually got married and moved to a big apartment in the city. Lovely place overlooking a park in the center of Copenhagen. We had many good friends and enjoyed it, but our purpose drove us. As a team, we got thousands of people introduced, and we got a lot of other Scientologists involved. Getting ordinary people interested was not only possible but easy.

Despite years of persistent romance, Trine had not conceived again. At the time, I had seen many miracles using L. Ron Hubbard's techniques; even I was a wandering miracle.

Trine and Christoffer 1989.

But I did not know that it could affect things like pregnancy. After receiving unique Scientology counseling about relationships, Trine got pregnant on the first attempt! There had been no other physical interventions, nothing but the cognitive interventions, then bingo!

It was a wonderful surprise for us and provided great happiness to Trine. The proof walks around now. His name is Christopher, and as of this writing–he is 32 years old.

Publisher, Salesman & Golf

None Dare Call It Conspiracy is a book authored in 1978 by the American journalist Gary Allen. The book was written in English, but I thought it was incredible and wanted to share it with people in Denmark upon reading it. The problem was that I could not find a Danish publisher interested. At that time, it was a very unconventional book that stepped on some important people's toes. Not one to be stopped, I had a friend translate it and started my own publishing company.

When you wander around sort of aimlessly, as I did in the first part of my life, you do not have much energy for anything but yourself. When you wake up, you have the power to be concerned with other things; you suddenly see all the lovely people around you. But gaining a higher consciousness has a flip side too–you also see all the bad things more clearly.

With all the world's misery, I had to wonder: does it happen randomly, or do unknown forces and people control and exploit others? These were the questions I was asking myself at the time. In *None Dare Call It Conspiracy,* the author had no doubt that things were planned and controlled. He outlined all the details in the book, which had become a classic in describing conspiracy theories and opening people's eyes. Since then, countless books have been written on the subject, and now the data is all over the internet.

Unfortunately, much of the information is now so perverted that, in the end, you do not know what is true and what is false.

A good stable point is "follow the money." That is what Gary Allan did. He investigated who owned the weapons industry, the medicine industry, the media, and the oil industry.

Today, people talk loudly about a One World Government, or New World Order: an umbrella over all governments where certain influential people exert remote control. There is talk about limiting the population, having a world currency, and so forth. The madmen behind these ideologies have many things in common; one is that they are wealthy. Some call them the Banksters because they own the banks; Globalists is another term used. You can Google the theories today and find them online. Gary Alan was talking about it 50 years ago.

It is said that many people work for and with these people without knowing the master plan.

The book implied that these families have no scruples and will do anything to get their plans achieved. They are cynical and cold, but they take good care of their own. If you go against them, they may have you removed or neutralized.

I undertook an awareness campaign, and I was very much into it. I drove around to bookstores in Denmark and personally sold 3,000 copies, many of them to individuals. It was exciting but also a bit exhausting, constantly dealing with bad news.

Not many people could handle that information at the time. They continued to vote for the wrong leaders and politicians, and they still do.

You could say that I left the information campaign incomplete. But I had another information campaign, which was much more critical, so I focused more on Scientology as a tool for a greater understanding of life. When you get better, you want others to get better, so I decided to tell more people about it.

During this period, the company I worked for sold Sharp office machines, such as cash registers and photocopiers. They had talented salesmen all over the country. I had never worked as a salesman before and did not do well for the first three months, but I quickly became good at it as I got into it.

Niels Kjeldsen is playing golf in Morocco on King Hassan's golf course.

It turned out by the end of that first year, I became the best salesman on a national level and stayed on top every year until I resigned five years later.

While at Sharp, I started spreading the knowledge I had learned to the other salespeople, which the owner did not appreciate. He was a Seventh-Day Adventist. One day he pulled me aside and said, "We do not disseminate during work hours." The following year, when my sales figures again were the best, he asked if I could influence my colleagues just a little so that they could sell more.

He also offered me a job as a sales manager. I said thanks but no thanks. The sales manager made less than I did and worked many more hours. Then I told him I could not influence my colleagues without getting into what I had learned in Scientology. His response was, "Well, then, that's fine." From that point on, I disseminated to my heart's delight.

As a result, I got all the sales staff into a center on the Communication Course. That was before Trine had opened CC Mission. Unfortunately, the team in that center was not up to par. They wore scooter boots and very casual clothes. These salesmen were used to suits and more of a business style. One of them, a very good friend, hung on to it and did more services.

When I was doing motorbike racing, it was a standing joke that you could just take up golf instead of racing if you had a bad day. But how can golf compare to racing? It cannot.

Hillerod Golf club in Denmark.

But then again, in some ways, it does. Today I am the guy you find on the course, just like I was the guy on the dirt track years ago.

And I must say that hitting a golf ball clean, on the sweet spot, produces a particular sensation that is not like racing, but it keeps you coming back to the course.

After a holiday in England, I became hooked on golf, where we played on the minor courses. There are many opportunities to do it wrong and just a few ways to do it right and have a good game.

It is also a great sport where you can meet lots of people and laugh, mostly at yourself. Anyone can compete with others and make a game of it with a smart handicap system. Previously, I played a lot of handball, which was about firing the ball off.

Of course, everything in golf is almost the opposite. Your movements must be perfectly synchronized in a smooth motion with the right timing.

One of the most famous golf holes, # 17 at Sawgrass in Florida.

One good discipline about golf that applies to everything in life, if you are unable to forget about the previous hit, things can go completely wrong on the next shot. You always must be in the moment. And there is no room for excuses.

I have seen many people trying to convince themselves that their lousy hit was the fault of others, or the course conditions, etc. If that does not work, you can always blame the clubs.

Of course, making excuses does not work because then everything really goes off the rails, and your game only goes down from there.

I love sports, and today probably spent way too much time watching Soccer, Speedway, and Formula One.

Effective Management Service

When it was new and rapidly growing, L. Ron Hubbard developed and created a simple and intelligent management technology for Scientology.

In the beginning, he had contacted many professionals who had been successful in management and asked them to take care of the organizational end of things so he could continue his research.

He quickly discovered that there was no uniformly workable technology in the field. It was very hit and miss. Just a few successful actions were not good enough for the expansion goals.

Mr. Hubbard decided to address the problems of management, and after more than three decades of research, piloting and codification, his body of knowledge on the subject comprises the world's most comprehensive system of management and represents the first consistently workable technology based on natural laws in the field. This management technology, though primarily designed for Scientology organizations, found extreme popularity and demand for it in the secular business world.

Thus WISE® was developed.

Niels Kjeldsen's car in 1997, Denmark.

WISE is a membership organization made up of entrepreneurs, business executives and professionals from every corner of every continent on Earth. WISE serves to unite all individuals and organizations that use Hubbard Administrative Technology in the world of commerce. (3)

The management system consisted of organizing boards, efficiency training, planning tools, a financial system, and much more.

One day I got the idea that it could be fun to get these Hubbard management tools out to the Danish business community. My company, Effective Management Service, was born.

It was an exciting and educational time for me. I started at home in my apartment, surveying businesspeople on the phone what they thought they most needed and wanted to succeed in business. I offered a free evaluation of their business to thank you for participating in the survey.

The answers from the surveys provided what I needed to know to market my company. When I met with a business owner and evaluated their business, I could sell them the Hubbard management course they needed most, according to what their business showed on the assessment. At first, I worked all alone. Then I got a person to help with phone appointments. Gradually the company grew.

After a few years as a small but effective business, I got a partner. He could make something happen, and suddenly we were ten people with a big office in an upscale place in Copenhagen. A few more years went by with lots of fun and significant challenges.

Then I had the pleasure of delivering the Communication Course to business people in Denmark that gave me such significant gains in 1976. We got our clients to think of good examples related to their business before each exercise, and after two days full time, you could see significant changes in these executives. Clients would write a success story about their progress as part of the course completion. We had given them a test before and after to ensure improvements.

Ole Boskov, musician and supervisor in Effective Management Service.

There were good gains every single time. Often the client would refer in more employees to do the same course. We quickly learned to always start with the boss because people would follow under them.

Ole, my partner, and I simultaneously supervised six or eight business executives on a course. Ole was also a musician and would play music for the students during the breaks. We delivered communication courses to many business people, and several of them also did efficiency training afterward. The changes that would happen with our clients after just two days were impressive. Many of them would be blown away. They got something for their money!

The efficiency training was about getting clients to clean up their tasks by writing down and completing all unfinished cycles of action.

"A cycle-of-action is start-change-and-stop. This parallels another cycle-of-action which is that of life itself. The cycle-of-action of life is: Creation-Survival-and-Destruction." L. Ron Hubbard. (4)

Often people start things, then before completing them, they drop the task and get onto another one. These unfinished tasks would stack up and cause unnecessary stress. As a result, the production and efficiency end up plummeting for both the executive and the company.

We would call the unfinished tasks backlogs. It would be pure dynamite for the business when we get the person to list and complete each of their incomplete cycles. Things would just "explode." Always in a good way, but sometimes it would get worse before it got better.

We typically sat with a customer for a full day. Sometimes it was new ideas that they started but did not carry through. Many business leaders face this indecisiveness daily.

They start something but never decide to follow through and complete it. That unfinished cycle just sort of floats in time. To help make decisions and get things fully completed, we taught our clients how to use this principle:

"Now, the basis of the individual is his ability to observe and make decisions and to act. And that is ability: his ability to observe, to make decisions, and to act." L. Ron Hubbard. (5)

It works great; if you cannot decide, you need to get more data, so when you have all the data, you can decide. And, of course, you then have to bring it to fruition. This is a dead-simple template that can help anyone in business and life.

Stinne and Christoffer in Florida 2004. (Daughter and son)

Many people have improved their lives by going through these intelligent but straightforward principles. Their companies progressed upward, and they became better and more efficient at their jobs. For us, it was a great way to live, help others and make money at the same time. I learned so much during that period. We had many satisfied customers. Several of them were interested to hear more about what Mr. Hubbard had done.

"All I beat the drum for is that the working worker deserves a break and the working manager deserves his pay and the successful company deserves the fruits of its success." L. Ron Hubbard. (6)

Villi

Trine's father, Villi, was a funny guy. At first, he was against what we were doing, but we spent a lot of time explaining it to him, and after a while, he could see the results we had, and he approved. Villi was the guy everyone listened to in the family, so it was time well spent to get him to understand.

When you practice techniques that help people, and help yourself, and have someone taking shots at what you do for no good reason, well, it is upsetting and disheartening at the same time. Should I or anyone who helps people have to listen to critical comments from someone who does not do anything to improve people? No!

After that, there was never a negative word again coming from Villi. Later, I was told that he became an ally and told people that Scientology was a good thing and his favorite child was doing it. He had done a complete about-face. He would not listen to any nasty comments himself. Sometimes, it snaps people out of their not-so-good game when you say it like it is.

Villi drank, smoked a ton, and ate unhealthily. He indulged in life, you could say. It finally all resulted in or contributed to a blood clot in his heart and several that followed.

He knew it was his time, and he listened intently to what I had to say about what he should do when the body died. But I had a perfect tip for him, and what I said and did with Villi is what is described in the last chapter of this book.

He was the first person I taught how to leave the body. The first test, you could say, worked perfectly. After leaving the body, he could get a communication through to me and say thank you for the help. He wanted to make sure that I got his message, which I did.

That incident was a big win because Villi did not know he was a spiritual being, just as many people don't know. Still, when his time came, he could grasp the concepts and make sure he didn't get lost and ended up exactly where he wanted after the body died. He managed it; others can do so too. They just have to follow the advice in the last chapter.

Once you have reached a certain spiritual level, one can go to the international center in Florida for the following higher levels. You do not have to live there, but we wanted to try something new. It was a big decision, but we wanted to move there relatively young. I sold my part of the company to my partner, so I had some money to start in the new place.

Trine had just reached her goal with CC Mission that she had started more than ten years earlier. She had built the place, and it was doing great. She turned over her responsibilities to other people.

It was time to go to the United States.

The Journey to America

The year 2000 was a significant change for the Kjeldsen family. Everything was new, and even though we had been to Florida a few times before, it was different when living here permanently. There are 22 million people in Florida alone, more than all the Scandinavian countries combined.

One of the top Scientology organizations globally is in Florida, where I now live. Since my business helps people avail themselves of the more advanced services, it is the perfect place for me.

Denmark was like your own backyard. You knew all the places and, of course, the language. You had things like the Queen's New Year's speech, the Christmas rice pudding, and this unique hotdog stand. None of that in the United States– but then again, the States has a lot more space, they think big, the cars are bigger, the gasoline is cheaper, and the burgers are unique. The only things we missed were our friends.

After a few years, I was able to get a Green Card for the whole family. Now I have US citizenship, dual citizenship in the US and Denmark.

Twilights in Florida

For Trine, living in the USA was a challenge in the beginning. She had worked day and night in Denmark, but she only worked a little here and there once in Florida.

After managing the center in Denmark, she had sworn that she would not do it again. Even though the rewards had been great, to open a center from scratch is a lot of work. But as the saying goes: "never say never." It didn't take long for Trine to realize her experience could also help many people in this area. So, just like that, she changed her mind and decided to start up a group.

There was a need for a place where ordinary people could stop shopping for a while and, under relaxed conditions, be introduced to Scientology. At that time, she did not have a green card and partnered with an American who could cover the legal stuff.

She found such a person, and in a short time, the new group was up and running, a place where Scientologists could bring their friends to hear a lecture or get involved in other introductory services.

After a year, the group was running full blast. I was also involved with it in many ways. The Americans liked her Danish accent and straightforward and relaxed ways of doing things. The rented place expanded fast. They got more rooms to meet the need. To this day, the center is still flourishing and continuing to grow.

All was going well for Trine and me. Our two children had become Scientologists on their own. Our son lived here in Florida with us, and our daughter got married and lived in Denmark. Little Emma was born, and we became grandparents. Everything was lovely. We could only see a bright future ahead.

There were a lot of places to experience, and we did that to a great extent. New York, the big city, was only a two-hour plane ride away. Disneyland was just around the corner in Orlando. Miami and Key West were within easy reach. We made great friends, and the weather was always good. We were happy with the decision we had made. People came here from all parts of the world, including many from Denmark. So, even though we were in a new place, there was familiarity as well.

Niels and his son Christopher in Florida 2004.

It is a good feeling when you create a future for yourself and cause it to happen. If you feel that you have no future, the feeling is the opposite, and that feeling came suddenly.

Trine got sick, or rather, she found out she was ill. We discovered she had stage four cancer. When it is that advanced, it means you have had it in the system for many years. An insidious, disgusting disease, as I see it, and it is unpredictable.

It seems to hit the best people; I only wish I knew why. Trine and I had been together for 25 years, so it was hard.

Nevertheless, we stayed positive. We took on the illness as a challenge worth conquering. "We will fix this" was our attitude, although the doctors were very skeptical. We were told people do not make it through that type of cancer. Then Trine will be the first, was our attitude. First came the chemo treatments.

After many treatments, however, her health did not improve. It got much worse. We tried several alternative therapies. We flew out to a skilled alternative doctor in Venezuela. He treated us so well, insisting not to charge anything for the treatment. A good friend had recommended him, and we got the complete VIP treatment. Later, we got our hands on yet another alternative medicine that had to be brought in from Ukraine.

After over a year of fighting, Trine gave up. She decided it was time to leave the body. Brave as she was, she called and informed friends and family in Denmark that she would not be here anymore in a few weeks.

Again, I had to use the procedure described in the last chapter of this book. But doing it with Trine was like a game, for she had already had several out-of-body experiences in her life. She knew she had lived before and would live again.

Once the decision was made, she wanted to go quickly. We thoroughly drilled what she should do after death, so she had complete control over it. Trine had always had confidence that I could help her through anything. In the end, I did help. Still, it was hard to say goodbye.

We could communicate after her body died, even though the communication was not the same as physical talk.

Perhaps what I am saying is unreal to you, but telepathic communication can happen after the body dies.

Trine and granddaughter Emma in 2005.

Believe it or not, it is something that you can practice. After Trine had departed her body, we were in communication with each other for a week.

Then she let me know it was time for her to leave and go where she had previously planned to be.

Because I had my negative and gloomy thoughts cleared with counseling before Trine died, it was easier to stay calm about her departure than it otherwise would have been.

But even in a good spiritual state, it is hard to go through the loss of someone so close. You would much rather see the ones you love live until ninety-five years old or more, which would be much easier to accept. At the date of this writing, Trine left us fifteen years ago.

Stinne and Niels, Florida 2006.

"God's Gift" to Niels Kjeldsen

Life was completely different after Trine was gone. At first, I didn't know what to do with myself, slumber or get lost in all sorts of tasks? Being in my mid-fifties, should I look for another mate? How would that be?

I would get invited to social affairs. Sometimes I would go, sometimes not. When you are used to going as a couple, it is bizarre to go alone.

But there was an invitation where I quickly said yes. A good friend was celebrating his 50th birthday in Thailand. I jumped on a plane from Tampa to Tokyo, from there to Bangkok and then Phuket, from there to one island and eventually by boat to another island, Ko Samui! I felt like I was at the end of the earth. But going there was well worth it. I went alone from the US and met all the other guests who had flown in from Denmark. The event was great fun. Thailand's culture is very different from Florida and Denmark. The experience goes into Niels's history book as an exciting one, primarily because of the return journey.

Oh man, what an experience. The tsunami hit the Tokyo coast as we were on the plane on the runway, getting ready to take off. Suddenly the plane shook. The passengers looked at each other in wonder. What the hell was that? A little later, the captain announced that he did not know what it was either, which didn't make us feel any better, trust me.

Ko Samui in Thailand 2011, with friends.

After what seemed like forever, sitting on the runway, the captain finally told us it had been an earthquake and then, bam, another shake! Neither the captain, Delta, or anyone else knew what to do. So, we just stayed there on the runway.

After a few hours of waiting, we went back to the terminal. While taxiing to the gate, the captain told us that all the terminal windows had been blown out and that they did not know what to do with us!

We spent a total of seven hours waiting on the plane without being served. We could not leave the aircraft. Finally, we were able to take off, and we were on the first flight out of Tokyo airport after the tsunami hit. At this point, we had a 9-hour trip to the US ahead of us.

No one was happy, but as we found out what had happened, everyone realized just how lucky we were. The tidal wave had hit the nuclear power plant and caused significant problems.

Ko Samui in Thailand 2011, with friends.

The 9.0 earthquake could be measured in Hawaii. When we arrived in the US, many diligent journalists waited at the airport to interview us. You can imagine that not many of us were in the mood after so many hours on the plane. I certainly was not. I just wanted to get in my bed!

I arrived home safe and sound and resumed my life. I was getting used to being alone. Then I met Theodosia. The name means God's gift to the people in Greek, and I immediately translated it into God's gift to Niels Kjeldsen. She was and still is beautiful, but would she be interested in a half-old man like me? Unexpectedly she was.

At that time, I was making regular trips back to Denmark, usually in the summer. When you get to July and August in Florida, it is hot and humid and a good time to leave. But in Denmark, it is usually a great time to be there. Theodosia lived in Copenhagen and spoke little Danish and fluent English. The following year she and I traveled back and forth to see each other. It was a great crush. A lot of love expressed both ways. She got the offer to move here to Florida. She has been here ever since.

It was as if life had just started again. To have a partner, you love and can communicate well with is vital.

Theodosia Kjeldsen, 2015.

I proposed on a cruise ship off the Bahamas; she said yes. We got married in Las Vegas, American style.

As one of my friends called her, Theodosia turned out to be a real go-getter. In only a few years, she had gone through almost all the steps available to one in Scientology. She was perfect for a dedicated person like me.

Theodosia is now an educated counselor and can provide just about anything a person needs to improve his or her life. It includes improving a person's self-confidence, gaining more energy, getting better at communicating, and having perseverance, and dealing with all those emotions that you do not like.

In other words, she can help people reach their potential in terms of happiness and productivity.

Theodosia partnered with another person that has a practice here in Florida. She is a star in her own right. She has much admiration for people and is a constant inspiration to people. She is loved by many people worldwide and is a great wife and partner for Niels.

Visiting Greece and the Greek archipelago with a native-like Theodosia is fantastic. More than once, she has taken me through the streets of Athens, as well as trips to Santorini and Mykonos. Greece has many proud people. Hopefully, the country will soon be liberated from the chains of the fat bankers.

Theodosia Kjeldsen in Florida.

In the next chapter, you will learn about what I have already presented to many people in Athens. They were highly interested to know it.

Today Theodosia and I are thriving as a couple and in life. We look forward to continuing to flourish and prosper.

I do everything I can to improve myself and others. It is what I am about. You are welcome to join the "club." I aim to tell everyone I can, what I have found to be true, and what works to enable people to attain a higher level of awareness

Niels and Theodosia Kjeldsen in the Greek Islands 2019.

Theodosia and Niels Kjeldsen.

What to do and what not do when you leave the body

The purpose of this chapter is to equip you with the knowledge to help others when it is time for them to leave the body or if they desire the information.

Many people throughout history have influenced others with incorrect information about the death. Opinion leaders in society, parents, religious teachers, and others that you had confidence in have likely fed you wrong information. It is no knock on you or who gave you the information. It is just a reality that must be acknowledged. That happens with other subjects, but especially the subject of death.

" SEEK TO LIVE WITH THE TRUTH.

False data can cause one to make stupid mistakes. It can even block one from absorbing true data. One can solve the problems of existence only when he has true data.

If those around one lie to him or her, one is led into making errors and his survival potential is reduced. False data can come from many sources: academic, social, professional.

Many want you to believe things just to suit their own ends.

What is *true* is what is true for you." L. Ron Hubbard. (7)

What I am about to present is not a theory. It is also not something you would learn in an American school or psychology class. I am offering knowledge that many individuals have used on a big scale time and again.

And although I say this, it still takes a little faith on your part; believe enough to listen to what is presented. Say and judge for yourself if you think it will help you and your loved ones.

There is the old analogy about a teacup representing knowledge. When the cup is full, you cannot add more tea (knowledge) to it. I am asking you to "empty your cup" so you have room for the knowledge I am about to impart.

"The Parts of man: THE INDIVIDUAL MAN is divisible into three parts. The first of these is the SPIRIT. The second of these parts is the MIND. The third of these parts is the BODY."
L. Ron Hubbard. (8)

The Body

It is an incredible machine. It is made of matter. It can heal itself and reproduce itself, and it offers many pleasures. But it does not go on forever. It is born. It lives a short or long time, then it stops. We could say it is born, survives, continues, and then goes into decay and dies.

The Mind

There are many varying ideas and definitions relating to the mind. If you ask five different people, "what is the mind," you might get five different answers—time to empty your cup.

I will give you a definition now that you can understand and one that you can use.

Of course, there is much more to learn on the subject, and good books explain it in detail, but this definition will do for now.

"The mind is a zone of pictures and the pictures contain perceptions.

"*Modern Science of Mental Health* describes the interrelationship of these pictures. Now, do you have a picture of a cat there? All right. Let me ask you this question now. Still have this picture of the cat now? Get that cat again. What's looking at the cat?"
L. Ron Hubbard. (9)

You can answer that question for yourself.

If I ask you to get a picture of where you went to grade school, you should be able to see that picture in your mind. Try it. Do you see it? A building? A classroom? What we are talking about here is your mind as mental pictures.

To what degree one can recall old pictures varies from person to person. It also varies how far you can go back in time. Many factors play into this. For now, it is enough to know that the mind consists of mental pictures that you can see.

One problem with the mind is that it can offer up pictures compulsively. It is problematic because when people have accidents, losses, and negative experiences, their minds store pictures of those incidents, which can later be triggered to impact the person negatively.

The Mind (pictures), the body, and the spirit. (the person)

The Spirit

Remember that picture of your grade school you looked at a moment ago? Close your eyes and look at it again. Now, ask yourself, what is looking at the picture?

There is a good chance that you will say I am! That is true. You are looking at the picture of the school. You are not the picture; you are the being (spirit) observing the picture.

Each individual knows the truth deep inside; it should not be too hard to accept this spirit definition. If you still have a hard time accepting this, then you can say to yourself, "Let us say that this is true," and then proceed from there. See for yourself if what I am about to present makes sense to you.

"Man thought he *had* a human spirit. No, that is totally incorrect-Man *is* a human spirit which is enwrapped more or less in a mind which is in a body. And that is Man, Homo sapiens, and he is a spirit and his usual residence is in his head and he looks at the pictures and the body carries him around." L. Ron Hubbard. (10)

The other thing to know about the spirit is that it is timeless. Whereas the body is made of matter, and only lives for so many years, the spirit (you) lives on. In other words, you continue to live on regardless of what happens to the body.

The big question is, how do you proceed after the body is gone, and can you decide where you want to end up and what you want to do the next time around? We are about to find out.

Photo shot by the artist Thorsten Overgaard.

Preparing for when the body dies

Almost 8,000 people die in the US every day. Worldwide more than 150,000 die and leave their body daily. Most of these people (spirits) come back in the next life more confused than before. If even a small percentage of these souls would do the steps described below, then this planet would eventually become a much calmer, more safe and saner place.

Said differently, just preventing the influences, stress, and lies that can be inflicted on people each time they die (between lifetimes) would improve planet Earth's condition. People would be in better shape, less confused when they come back.

Most people do not plan when they are going to move on. That is why you and your loved ones need to know the "landscape" in advance. If you heed the information here, you will end up where you decided to be the next time around and not any other place.

Additionally, you will be able to assist others by explaining what to do and not to do when they no longer can keep the body alive.

"But the first thing one learns about death is that it is not anything of which to be very frightened. If you're frightened of losing your pocketbook, if you're frightened of losing your memory, if you're frightened of losing your girl or your boyfriend, if you're frightened of losing your body, well, that's how frightened you ought to be of dying, because it's all the same order of magnitude."
L. Ron Hubbard. (11)

Now you are used to viewing the world through your body's eyes. Not only sight but all the sensations you have been experiencing is with the assistance of the body. We could say that your body has been a stable point in your life.

When you leave it, you suddenly get a different perception of things; it can be confusing. You have lost that stable point.

First, let's talk about what not to do

When you reach the end of your life and exit the body, it will not be the first time you have done so. It has happened countless times. This time I do not want you or the person you are assisting to have any *hidden influences*. These influences are one of the main reasons most people cannot remember their past lives.

When the body dies, you (the spirit) may feel an urge to go somewhere. It can be a compulsion expressed in different ways.

Do not be persuaded to do so, even if it feels proper and highly comfortable. These are traps designed to confuse you, so you end up in places you do not want to be. Do not be deceived; instead, you want to control where you end up.

"Very easy to forget about death because that's what death is, a forgettingness. However, we do have a considerable amount of information on this subject and you actually are entitled to that information." L. Ron Hubbard. (12)

What to do

Here is what to do to secure your future. I have presented it so that you could tell another how to proceed when the time comes. If you are the one assisting another, then go over the material covered earlier on Body, Mind, and Spirit.

If the person can still respond, find out if there is anything the person wants to complete before leaving. It can be unfinished actions they are involved in or even communication they wish to express to others.

Whatever the person says, do what you can to help them get it done. If the person wrote a will, it is essential to do what was asked for, including what to do with the dead body.

Cremation is recommended. It pretty much guarantees that after the person leaves the body, they will no longer be drawn to the body. It makes it easier for the person to start a new life.

At this point, the person has a good understanding of Body, Mind, and Spirit and has gotten his attention off the incomplete actions. Then you proceed as explained here. Here is an example:

"Where is a good place that you are very familiar with?" Person answers. My garden, the kitchen, the park, or whatever place the person is comfortable.

"Well now, where is a good place that you're very familiar with? Well, when you die, appear there. Now remember that. When you die, appear such-and-such a place." L. Ron Hubbard. (13)

"Okay. When you die, appear there!" Simply decide to appear at that place. Keep it as simple as described above.

It has to be a place that he/she is familiar and comfortable with, not what you think the person is familiar with or what you like. From experience, some people tend to tell people what they should believe and do, but the person, him/herself, must decide the place.

A person without a body, (the spirit in other words) does not travel to the place they decide to be. They just appear there. It is the nature of the spirit. You just decide you want to be somewhere, and you are there. It will happen once the person has *decided* fully to be there.

Your job is to ask about the place he or she is familiar and comfortable with and then tell him or her to show up there.

This method of just *being* at a place works. Telling another about this may just be the most significant help you will ever provide to someone.

After the person departs the body, do not be surprised if they send you a communication or a sign. Be open to receiving this, as it might be vital to get the message through. Often you will get a big "thank you."

What I am saying here is the fact. The procedure outlined above might seem real to you or not, but it works anyway.

Similar to you using your cell phone, it works whether you believe it or not. The phone will allow you to talk to anyone on earth. Not only that, but you can also see them talking to you on the screen.

Pass these data along to your loved ones. And when your time comes, as it will for all of us, follow the procedure. It is simple. Just do it and know that it is the right thing to do.

These data have been used repeatedly by chaplains and ministers educated in this material and by me. All have come to the same conclusion that the more direct and straightforward approach is better.

Most people are not in the best shape when you talk to them about this subject. Therefore, as little talk and discussion, the better.

A popular question people ask is, "After I depart my body and I am there, at the place where I decided to be, then what?"

The truth is that people can do what they want to do at that point. But remember that we have all departed a body before, gotten a baby body, and started a new life. We have done it many times. Therefore, when the time comes, and the person is where they want to be, you have done an excellent job.

Before anything else, the individual can look around in this new condition as a being. Get used to perceiving things as a spirit and take it from there.

To help a person before they leave their body, all you need to do is impart the information in this book.

If you have any questions, I would love to hear from you. You can contact me on my website: nielskjeldsen.com.

"Just as every death begins new life, so does every failure eventually challenge forth new attempt until death itself is reached. Actually, both failure and death alike are transient. They are educational building blocks on a much longer road."
L. Ron Hubbard. (14)

Bibliography

1. L. Ron Hubbard, Scientology Booklet on Communication

2. L. Ron Hubbard, from the book Creation of Human Ability

3. WISE, from WISE invitation letter

4. L. Ron Hubbard, from the book The Problems of Work

5. L. Ron Hubbard, from lecture 3 April 1962

6. L. Ron Hubbard, WISE, Executive Basic Workshop booklet

7. L. Ron Hubbard, The Way to Happiness booklet

8. L. Ron Hubbard, from the book Fundamentals of Thought

9. L. Ron Hubbard, from Dear Alice Lectures, 16 May 1957

10. L. Ron Hubbard. from lecture Death 30 July 57

11. L. Ron Hubbard, from lecture Death 30 July 57

12. L. Ron Hubbard, from lecture Death 30 July 57

13. L. Ron Hubbard, from lecture, 23 July 1963

14. L. Ron Hubbard, from the book Handbook for Preclears

Niels Kjeldsen:

Danish and American Citizen, living in the USA.

Married to Theodosia Kjeldsen.

Father to two grown-ups. One grandchild.

Personal and spiritual counselor.

Founder of two different companies.

Won several championships in sidecar racing in the seventies.

Art and sports enthusiast.

Author of the book "How to survive Death."

Photo copyright by the photographers:

Thorsten Overgaard: Page 27, 60, 65, 66, 99, 100, 103, 105, 110,113, 117

Asbjorn Christiansen (AC): Page 18, 42.

Horst Dubiel: Page 109

Niels Kjeldsen: Page 7, 10, 12, 15, 20, 22, 24, 25, 30, 31, 32, 33, 36, 37, 38, 39, 44, 45, 49, 53, 55, 57, 62, 69, 71, 72, 74, 78, 80, 81, 83, 85, 87, 91, 93, 96,97, 101,104.

Printed in Great Britain
by Amazon

17564852R00068